16 Duets for Bass Clef Instruments (Trombone, Euphonium and others)

Two For Easter

James Curnow

CURNOW® MUSIC

Order Number: CMP 1139-06-401

James Curnow
Two For Easter
Bass Clef Instruments

ISBN-10: 90-431-2566-0
ISBN-13: 978-90-431-2566-6

Two For Easter

Sixteen Unaccompanied Duets for Easter
For any instruments

Easter Greetings!

Music at Easter is an extremely important part of celebrating this most wonderful time of year. As we celebrate the resurrection of our Lord, music adds much joy to the celebration.

These easy duets are designed to allow the average to advanced players the opportunity to perform in church, school, or anywhere Easter is being celebrated. No accompaniment is necessary. They may be played by any combination of woodwind, brass, string or mallet percussion instruments.

Below is an instrumentation guide that tells you the appropriate book to purchase for your instrument. For example, an instrument in C may combine with an instrument in B♭, E♭, F, Bass Clef or any Mallet Percussion instrument, or a B♭ instrument may combine with instruments in C, B♭, F, Bass Clef or any Mallet Percussion instrument, etc. by purchasing the books in the appropriate key.

Most of all have fun and join in the celebration.

James Curnow
Composer/arranger

Instrumentation Guide

<u>C Instruments</u> (CMP 1135-06-401)   Piccolo, Flute, Oboe, Violin, or any Mallet Percussion instrument.

<u>B♭ Instruments</u> (CMP 1136-06-401)   Clarinet, Bass Clarinet, Comet, Trumpet, Flugel Horn,
Tenor Saxophone (play first part only), Trombone T.C.,
Euphonium/Baritone T.C., Tuba T.C. (play second part only).

<u>E♭ Instruments</u> (CMP 1137-06-401)   Alto Clarinet, Alto Saxophone, & Baritone Saxophone (play
second part only), Tuba T.C. (play second part only).

<u>F/E♭ Instruments</u> (CMP 1138-06-401)   F/E♭ Horn

<u>Bass Clef Instruments</u> (CMP 1139-06-401)   Cello, Double Bass (play second part only), Bassoon,
Trombone B.C., Euphonium/Baritone B.C., Tuba B.C.
(play second part only).

Table of Contents

B.C. INSTRUMENT

TWO FOR EASTER

Arr. **James Curnow** (ASCAP)

1. CHRIST AROSE

Robert Lowry

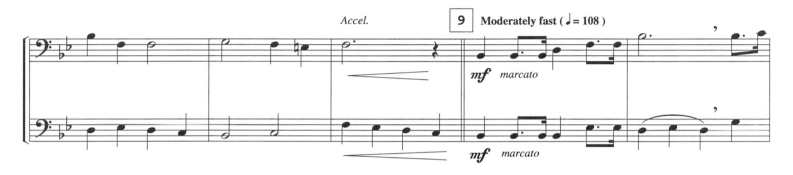

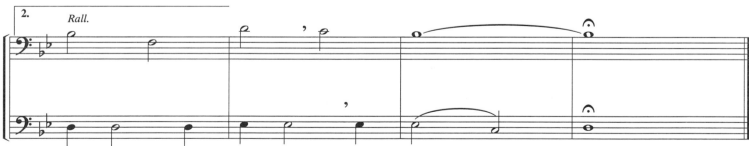

2. CROWN HIM WITH MANY CROWNS
(Diademata)

George J. Elvey

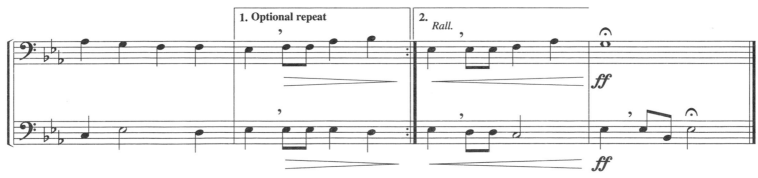

3. O SACRED HEAD, NOW WOUNDED

Hans L. Hassler

(Passion Chorale)

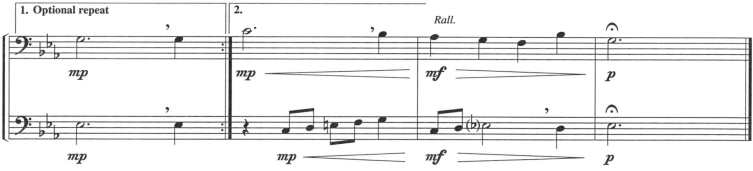

4. COME YE FAITHFUL, RAISE THE STRAIN
(St. Kevin)

Arthur S. Sullivan

5. CHRIST THE LORD IS RISEN TODAY

(Easter Hymn)

from *Lyrica Davidica*

6. WERE YOU THERE?

Traditional

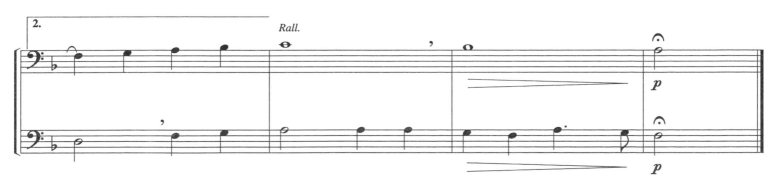

7. LO! HE COMES IN CLOUDS DESCENDING
(Sicilian Hymn)

Henry T. Smart

8. REJOICE, THE LORD IS KING
(Darwall)

John Darwall

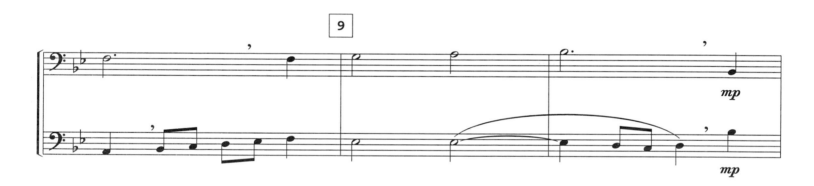

9. FAIREST LORD JESUS

From *Schleische Volkslieder*

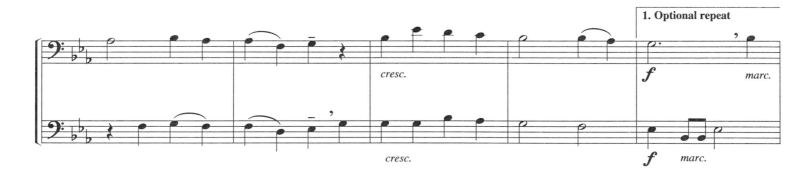

10. REJOICE, YE PURE IN HEART

Arthur H. Messiter

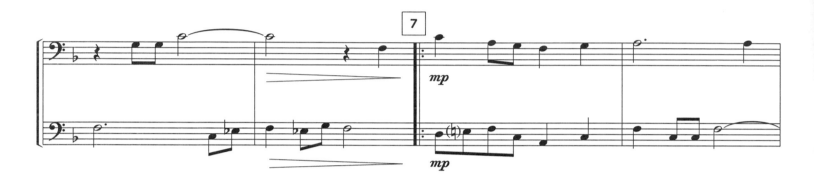

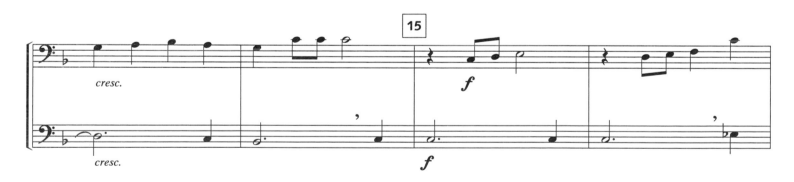

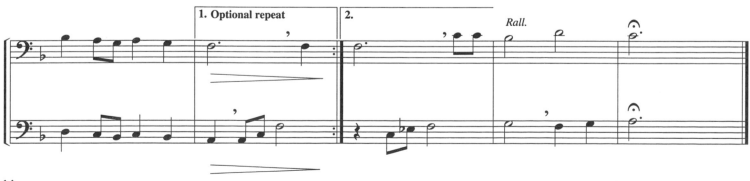

11. ALL HAIL THE POWER OF JESUS NAME
(Coronation)

Oliver Holden

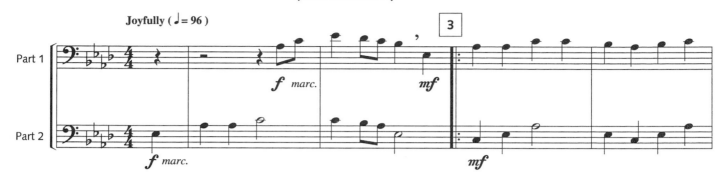

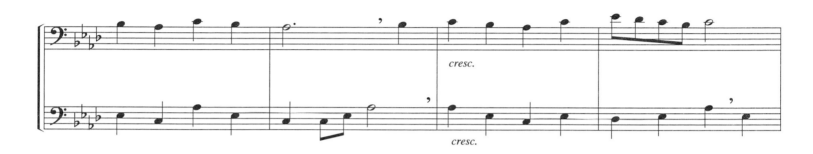

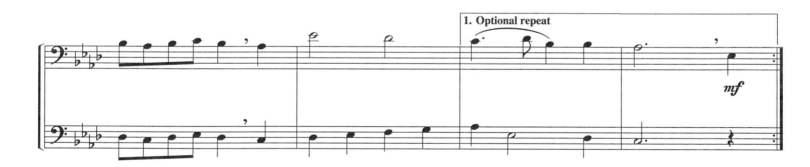

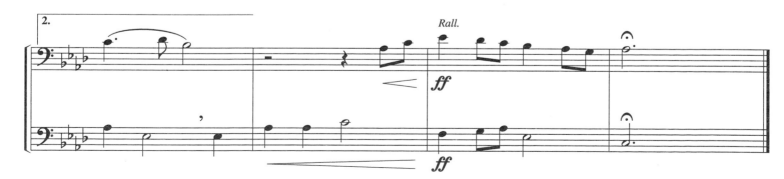

12. THINE IS THE GLORY
(Judas MacCabeus)

George F. Handel

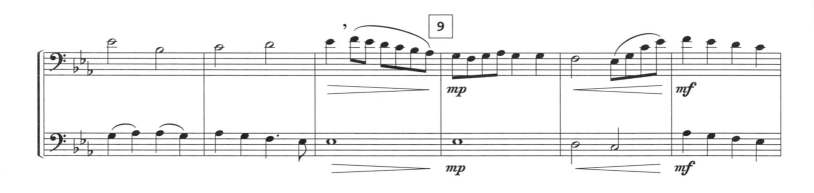

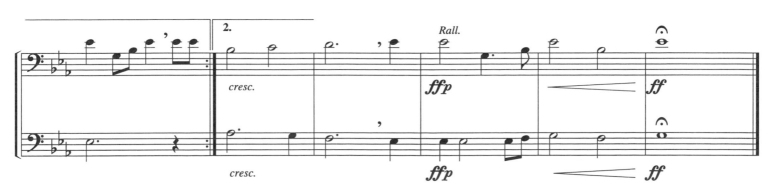

13. JESUS SHALL REIGN
(Duke Street)

John Hatton

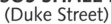

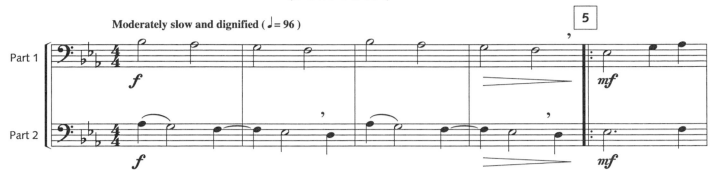

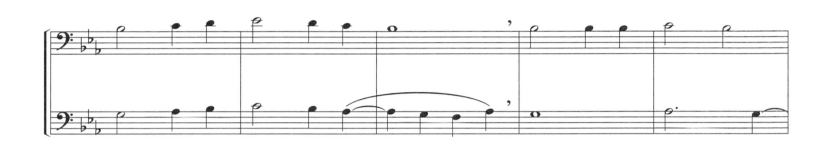

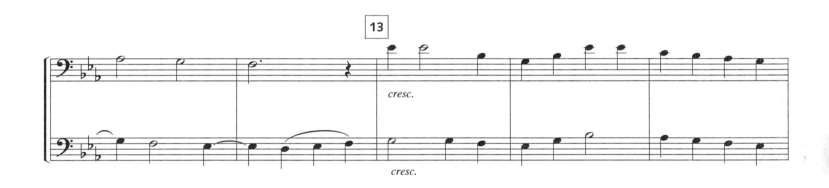

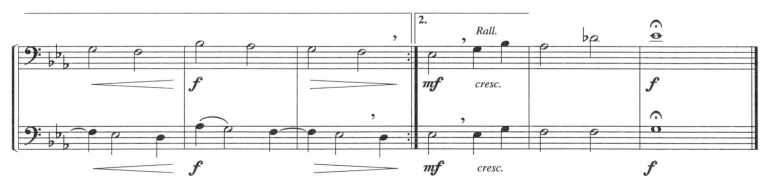

14. COME, THOU ALMIGHTY KING
(Italian Hymn)

Felice de Giardini

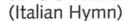

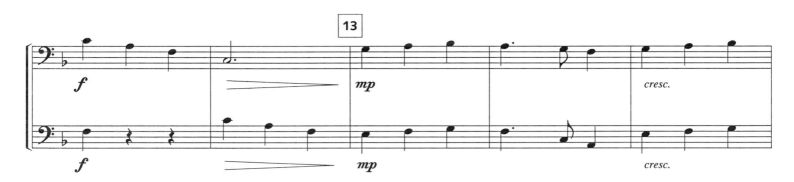

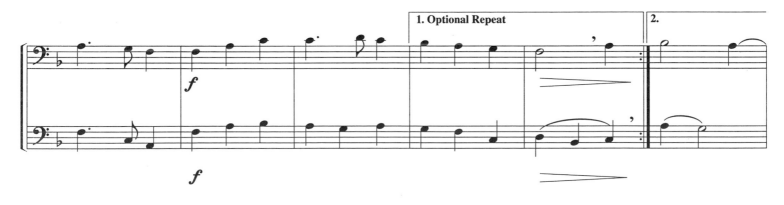

15. AT THE CROSS

Ralph Hudson

16. COME, CHRISTIANS, JOIN TO SING

Traditional